PHOTOGRAPHS BY MARTHA SWOPE

Ballet Is the Best Exercise

by

CYNTHIA GREGORY

with Kathy Matthews

SIMON AND SCHUSTER NEW YORK

To JWH for the dreams and to HBM for the realities.

Library of Congress Cataloging-in-Publication Data
Gregory, Cynthia.
    Ballet is the best exercise.
    1. Ballet dancing.   2. Exercise.   I. Matthews,
Kathy, date.   II. Swope, Martha.   III. Title.
GV1788.G69   1986   792.8'2   86-15525
ISBN: 0-671-54459-4

ACKNOWLEDGMENTS

Working on this book with Kathy Matthews was such a joy: It was also a new and interesting experience for me and I'd like to thank a few women who helped along the way.

Susan Cook from Martha Swope's studio was so generous with her time and expertise, as was Alice Galloway, stage manager for American Ballet Theatre. She videotaped me demonstrating every bit of my material so that Kathy could watch it over and over for the finer points.

And of course there is Susan Victor, the editor of this book. She has guided me through this entire project from its inception with quiet suggestions, a wealth of experience, and lots of enthusiasm. I feel that Kathy and I were a match made in heaven, and it was Susan Victor who brought us together. She was aided by many fine people from Simon and Schuster, including Eve Kirch, the designer, and Leslie Ellen, the copy editor.

To me, books are such treasures, and to have created my first one, with the assistance of all these lovely people, has me glowing with pride and satisfaction.

CONTENTS

Part Two: The Exercises

Part Three: The Dance

INTRODUCTION

Ballet has always been the only exercise for me. From the time I was a little girl, I wanted nothing more than to be a ballerina.

I started to take ballet lessons on the advice of my doctor when I was five years old. As I was very susceptible to colds and flu, he suggested that regular exercise would build my strength. My mother loved ballet—she's very musical—and she enrolled me in a weekly class. Soon I was studying four or five times a week with several good teachers and performing with local ballet groups. I even danced with Jack Benny on TV and in a movie with Jane Powell!

When I was fourteen years old the San Francisco Ballet came to town. I auditioned for, and received, a Ford Foundation Scholarship to study at their school. Ballet was changing my life and my parents' lives too. On the first day of 1961 we all moved to San Francisco. I realize now how fortunate I was to have such loving and supportive parents. I was their only child and they gave up their comfortable lives in Los Angeles in order to further my opportunities in the dance world. They believed in my talent right from the very beginning.

By the time I was fifteen, I was a full-fledged member of the San Francisco Ballet Company. But my dream was to dance with a major company in New York, and so when I was nineteen I left San Francisco for New York City. I was accepted in the American Ballet Theatre in July of 1965. Almost a year later I was promoted to soloist and, after making my debut as the Swan Queen in *Swan Lake* in April 1967, I became a principal dancer. I'm still performing with ABT; after more than twenty years I guess it will always be my "home" in the dance world.

To be honest, when I first began dancing, and indeed through my early career, I never thought about the physical benefits of ballet. I was more concerned with the thrill of performing and the pleasure of making my body do beautiful things. In that respect, dance has been a very rewarding career for me. I've performed all over the world and have been partnered by all the great male dancers of our time, including Nureyev, Bruhn, Baryshnikov and Bujones. I've received dance awards, appeared on television specials like the "Night of a Hundred Stars," and even done a commercial for American Express. But in recent years I've come to appreciate another aspect of ballet—its physical benefits—the reason I took it up so many years ago. After all, ballet has kept me strong, healthy and feeling young, and I've come to value it as exercise with both an extraordinary appeal and an extraordinary effectiveness.

Ballet is a system, developed over centuries, whose goal is to strengthen the body while molding it to an ideal of grace and beauty. It's enjoyable—even exhilarating—effective and, if done correctly, safe. It gives you all the cardiovascular benefits of aerobic exercise, but ballet also helps to develop fluidity of movement and poise as no other exercise can. And it's the only exercise that allows you to look good while you're doing it as well as afterward.

There is a special aspect to ballet that I think is important—it's safe. Safety is a factor that is sometimes ignored in exercise routines. Straight-legged sit-ups, quick head rolls, and any number of other exercises can pull muscles, strain your body and sometimes cause serious injury. No one is more aware of these problems than a dancer. A ballerina's body is her instrument, and she must protect it from injury at all costs. A pulled tendon, a ripped muscle, can mean days and weeks of frustrating recovery. I've always been particularly afraid of a snapped tendon, as that is such a graphic and frightening accident. If ever I were tempted to skip a warm-up, the thought of a snapped tendon would surely scare me into it! I have been injured, of course. Once in a performance my partner lifted me too quickly and my hip was thrown out. The resulting torn muscle kept me from dancing for more than four months.

I developed the exercises in the first part of this book myself and have used them for years to warm up before class and before performances. When I arrive at a theater for a performance, I have to put on my costume and my makeup; there's no formal warm-up for the dancers. So we all can be seen backstage in various stages of dress going through the personal warm-up routines that we've each developed over the years. We're faithful to these routines because we can do them quickly and easily any time or place. The routines in this book—my personal routines—are not just for dancers or for people who want to do a series of dance exercises; they can be used as exercises in their own right or as a warm-up for any kind of activity—tennis, jogging, basketball, for example—anything that requires your body to be limber so as to avoid strain and injury. This kind of a warm-up is crucial to a professional dancer and it should be to you too. You'll find a good warm-up will enable you to work better and to perform your activity with more control and finesse.

Ballet has by its very nature a built-in safety factor. Dancers don't exercise lying on the floor or sitting on a machine or handling weights. They are standing, bending, reaching and turning—all everyday, natural movements. In ballet your body is always under control. Control is the essence of ballet. It's this constant control, even while doing seemingly effortless movements, that develops strength and endurance. At the same time, control prevents strain and injury.

The fact that all of the movements of ballet are natural movements gives ballet exercise another advantage: It brings grace to your everyday movements. Ballerinas are not only graceful when they dance; they're graceful when they sit, stand and walk. In fact, you can often pick a dancer out of a crowd because of her poise. This is because ballet is a total exercise. It works the whole body—head, arms, legs, hips and torso—constantly. No one body part is emphasized at the expense of another because the goal is appearance as well as movement and strength. Consciousness of the total body working as a graceful unit is a habit than can be learned, and ballet exercises will make everyday grace a natural habit.

Ballet is also remarkably effective at shaping your body. Ballet emphasizes long, lithe muscles and it helps to create them. In Russia, the physical proportions of ballet students are measured at various times and only those students conforming to the ideal survive as dancers. But in the United States there are many top ballerinas who have proven that determination, along with regular work, can shape a less-than-perfect body into an instrument of graceful perfection. The average woman can gain the same benefits from ballet exercise. Most women are not interested in building large muscles. They want to be firm, toned and sleek. There's nothing better than ballet for creating today's ideal body.

There's an unfortunate misconception today about the "ballet body." People, especially women, tend to think that if they're not tall and thin, there's no point in trying ballet. In fact, the trend for tall, thin dancers is a very recent phenomenon that can be attributed largely to Balanchine and the dancers he preferred for the New York City Ballet. In the past, ballet dancers were most commonly short and, if not fat, then not exactly thin either. I remember being amazed when I first saw photos of early ballerinas. They were small and strong and sometimes absolutely plump. It's always been important to have a body that's in proportion, but if you're not tall and willowy don't think you can't enjoy ballet. Indeed, some moves are best executed by short dancers: jumps, for example, usually look much better when done by a short dancer. A tall, loose dancer seems to take too long to get into the air and too long to come down. A short dancer, like Baryshnikov, is so compact and strong that he can make wonderful high, clean jumps. So don't let your height or body build keep you from ballet.

There's one last thing about ballet as an exercise that I think is special. It's the same thing that first appealed to me as a child when I watched my first performance: It looks wonderful. And it doesn't only look wonderful on the stage. The exercises and movements of ballet are designed to look good; it is, after all, a visual art. Women look beautiful when they're doing ballet exercises. The movements are fluid. The music is delightful. There is a readily available assortment of leotards, leg-warmers, dance skirts and soft dance shoes that are wonderfully flattering and make any woman feel graceful and pretty. The whole atmosphere of ballet and ballet warm-ups and exercises is romantic.

I really do think that ballet is the best exercise, and I hope that once you try it you'll agree.

PART ONE

The Basics

Posture

Good posture—the correct line of the body, called "alignment" in ballet —is absolutely crucial if you want to get the most out of the ballet exercises. After all, from one point of view, ballet is simply correct posture in motion. I can't emphasize this enough and, in fact, I recommend that you do all the exercises very, very slowly at first so you can concentrate on your posture and the correct placement of your arms, legs, hips, head and torso.

All of the ballet exercises—with one minor exception—start the very same way: with a certain stance that you would immediately identify as that of a ballerina. For my exercises you don't need the absolute precision of the professional dancer, but you do need to learn how to stand like a dancer. Learning how to stand and hold yourself properly takes effort at first, but it will soon become second nature. And it's only by learning to work in the correct position that you will really experience the benefits and beauty of these exercises. You need to become conscious of every part of your body and these exercises will help you develop that kind of awareness.

The biggest misconception about a ballerina's posture is that it is exaggerated. To the contrary, it is really a natural, good posture and only the positions of the feet—which we're not going to bother with—are extreme. Once this good posture comes automatically, not only will you be exercising correctly, but you'll also find that you stand and move with more grace and ease.

Keep in mind that your movements and positions should feel and look natural. The French have a phrase "to feel good in your skin." When you do these exercises, you must feel good in your skin. If you are sticking your fanny out or holding your arms stiffly, you will feel awkward and look that way too. No, you must feel graceful, even, indeed especially, when you're working your hardest.

Some people find metaphors helpful to give them an image of how they should move and feel. I agree that physical metaphors can be enormously useful. But they can also backfire. For example, I've watched children at a dance class who have been told to think of themselves as flying. They usually begin to stiffen their arms slightly and flap with enthusiasm. A similar problem occurs when the little ones imagine themselves as flowers in the spring breeze. Soon you have a roomful of little dancers swaying their stems and they've entirely lost control of everything but their hips and their ankles.

I had a teacher in Los Angeles, Carmelita Maracci, who used some of the most beautiful and effective images that I've ever heard. She's an extraordinary teacher, and I still come to her classes when I'm in L.A. because her classes, which she choreographs to wonderful music, are an inspiration to all her students. Her images are memorable, maybe in part because they're so simple. For example, she tells us to let our hands fall as if they were leaves in a slight wind, now held aloft, now trembling, now moving to the ground. There is a movement called *rond de jambe* where you move your foot in a semi-circle on the floor, and she tells us to move our legs as if they were oars moving through water. And when we get stiff and awkward she reminds us not to hold our arms as if they were coat racks.

I have found one useful metaphor that emphasizes the subtle upward thrust and graceful but deliberate movement of the body that is so impor-

tant to ballet. Think of yourself as a puppet. Every joint of your body has a string attached to it and someone is manipulating your limbs. But you're not an ordinary puppet with jerky movements. You're under water! Every movement you make is slowed by the weight of the water that presses you down. You move smoothly but not without effort. Sometimes you move quickly but always the water resists you so there are no jerks, no snaps. Everything is fluid. If you keep the underwater puppet in mind, you may find that your own body will instinctively move in the right way.

The Feet

When you align your body for an exercise, you begin with your feet. Your feet and their proper positioning are the foundation for all your exercises. Dancers' feet take a lot of punishment and they look it. Most of us have bunions and lumps and even slight deformities. This is because we do so much work on our toes. Many people have a second toe that's longer than their big toe and that means when they work on pointe—or on their toes—that single second toe is supporting all their weight. You can see why that could cause problems. I've been lucky in this regard because even though I started working on pointe at the age of eight—much too early!—my toes are almost straight across and so my weight was

supported over a broad base. Of course you won't have such problems because we won't be doing any work on pointe, but nonetheless you must learn how to place your feet correctly.

First your feet much be relaxed. That means you don't grab the floor with your toes. Your toes are flat and most of the weight of your body should be resting on three spots: your heel, your little toe and your big toe.

Be careful not to let your ankles roll in or out. Ankles out of alignment will throw off the line of your whole body and could result in a strained muscle. You may feel an impulse to let your ankles roll in or out when you go up on your toes, but guard against it. To strengthen your feet and ankles you can sit in a chair, extend one leg at a time and slowly, slowly point your toe, keeping your foot as straight as you can. I do this little exercise frequently while watching TV. You can also practice holding a support with both hands and going up on the balls of your feet. Put a mirror in front of your feet so you can be sure that your ankles are straight and your weight correctly distributed across the ball of each foot.

Turnout

For all the exercises but one, you will begin by standing with your feet slightly turned out. In classical ballet we turn our feet out to an ideal angle of 180 degrees. The whole leg rotates from the hips. It takes a great deal of practice to achieve this turnout, but it's not necessary or even desirable for the exercises in this book. I've designed these exercises for the average person who hasn't studied classical ballet and I've taken into account the turnout position of the beginner. If you try to exaggerate your turnout you will likely find yourself out of alignment and straining, even injuring, muscle, especially the muscles of your ankles and feet, which are particularly vulnerable.

Here's how to find the turnout that's correct for you. Stand holding on to a support with your left hand, your heels about an inch apart. Turn your toes out, rotating your legs at the hip, as far as you comfortably can without losing your alignment. Remember that your body should never be stiff. Your feet must still be carrying your weight on three points: the big toe, little toe and heel. Your ankles must be straight and your knees should be just above your feet. If your bottom sticks out or tucks too far under, you're probably turned out too far. Remember that your body must be relaxed and free to move easily.

Legs

If your posture is good and your feet are placed correctly, your legs will be placed properly. Here's how they should be as you begin. Your knees should be straight, but never lock them or force them back. Your knees should point in the same direction as your toes. To check that they do, you can bend them slightly, keeping your feet flat on the floor. They should move directly toward your toes.

You should feel the muscles in your thighs pulling up and there should be a slight tension, but never stiffness, in those muscles.

Torso

To get your torso into proper alignment you've got to focus on your rib cage, tummy and bottom. Most people have trouble getting their bottoms into line. They tend to create a swayback by curving the spine so that the bottom sticks out or they tuck in the tummy so tightly that the pelvis is tipped forward.

I think the best way to get your torso into alignment is to lift your rib cage by inhaling and expanding your chest and shoulders, and then tightening your abdominal muscles and slimming your waist. If you do these two things, and then just slightly tense your buttocks, your bottom should fall into correct alignment. If you put one hand flat on your tummy and the other flat on the small of your back, both hands should be nearly parallel (with the back hand curving in slightly) and perpendicular to the floor.

Whatever you do, don't stick out your fanny, as this will throw off your whole body and give you a ducky waddle. Many people tend to arch the back, which pushes out the bottom and inhibits freedom of movement. The duck position can also cause injury because it forces you to use the wrong muscles.

Always remember to pull up from the waist while keeping your shoulders down, and your torso will fall into alignment. If you imagine that you have a string attached to your breastbone that is pulling your chest upward, you'll achieve the open, lifted look and feeling.

Arms and Hands

When you do your ballet exercises, you'll be using your arms and hands for balance and for grace.

As far as balance is concerned, using your arms in the correct position can help steady you when you do certain movements, especially when you have a foot lifted off the floor. But the main objective in the positioning of the arms is to achieve a graceful line.

The most important thing to remember as you hold and move your arms in these exercises is that they should always be slightly curved, never completely straight. That's true for the hands as well as the arms. The elbow shouldn't be stiff but should be very slightly bent forward. The hand should continue that curve.

Many people have difficulty holding their hands properly. They tend to make the fingers rigid and stiff. Here's a trick that helps find the right, relaxed hand position for you: Hold your arms in front of you, elbows bent, and shake your hands a few times as if you were shaking down a thermometer in each hand. Then simply stop shaking. Your fingers, if they are really relaxed, will fall into the correct position, and so will your hand, with the wrist slightly bent down by the weight of the hand itself. Think of the puppet string attached to the top of your wrist; the rest of the hand is relaxed.

Keep in mind as you hold and move your arms that while they shouldn't be stiff, they should never be limp. There must always be a certain amount of muscular tension in them.

When your arms are extended directly in front of you or to the side, they should be held at just below shoulder height and—this is absolutely crucial, whether your arms are at waist level, extended to the side or lifted above your head—you must never allow your shoulders to be raised or thrown out of line. Your shoulders must always be held down. This can be difficult to achieve. Especially when you lift your arms, you'll feel like lifting your shoulders too. But don't! If you lift your shoulders you won't be working the correct muscles and you lose your look of graceful control. When you keep your shoulders level you may feel a bit of a pull in the joint as you move the arms, but eventually your shoulder will become more flexible.

Head

It is very desirable for a dancer to have a long neck because it adds a lissome extended line to the body. But even dancers without the enviable "swan" neck create the impression of having one by always lengthening the line of their necks and holding their heads high. Any woman can make her neck appear longer by holding her head high as she keeps her shoulders down. Just be careful to keep your neck relaxed and don't stick your chin out—keep it parallel to the floor. Remember that the imaginary puppet string that is holding up your head is attached to the top of your head, not your chin.

Starting Position Checklist

Each exercise except one begins from the same starting position, which is a simple standing position with your arms held slightly in front of your thighs and your feet, heels nearly touching, slightly turned out. It's simple, but it's important to get it right.

- **Feet:** For most of the exercises, heels are placed about an inch apart and toes are turned out as far as is comfortable. In the other exercises, the feet are parallel, an inch or two apart.
- **Legs:** The leg muscles, particularly those in the thighs, are pulling upward.
- **Torso:** The chest is lifted, stomach pulled in, and bottom is neither too tucked in nor too stuck out.
- **Head:** The neck is long, chin forward but not stuck out.
- **Arms:** The arms are slightly curved at the elbow and wrist, the hands a few inches in front of the tops of the thighs. The hands are curved and graceful, not stiff, palms facing each other. The shoulders are down.

The Plié

The plié is a basic ballet move and, as you'll be using it in a number of the exercises, it would be helpful to understand exactly how it should be performed.

Basically a plié involves bending the knees and lowering the torso while keeping the upper body straight. Sometimes you'll do a plié with your heels together, sometimes with your feet 12 inches or so apart. In either case, your bent knee should remain directly over your foot. The basic position of your upper body, which I've already described, does not alter as your knees bend. It's important to keep your head high, your chest lifted and your back straight. One of the biggest troubles people run into with the plié is that they either arch their backs or curve forward. Either one will throw off the line of your plié. If your back is straight and your chest out, your bottom will fall into place without sticking out or tucking in too far.

The plié is an exercise that increases the strength and flexibility of your legs. Your legs are really doing the work in a plié, especially your thighs. You should do the plié with a consciousness of those taut leg muscles. Don't just let your body sink as your knees bend; feel the strength of your thighs as you slowly lower yourself into a plié. Also, as you straighten your knees and come up from a plié, don't bounce up. Rather, move slowly, feeling the energy in your legs as you lift your upper body.

I suggest that you practice a few pliés, watching yourself in profile in a mirror, if possible. From the side you can see if your knees are above your feet, if your back is straight, and if your bottom is in just the right position.

Breathing

Breathing correctly while you exercise is more important than you may think. The way you breathe affects the look and line of your body. You can readily see this if you stand in a leotard before a mirror. Notice that when you lift your chest and breathe deeply, your spine is lengthened and your waist slimmed.

But of course you don't breathe for appearances' sake only! In order to have enough oxygen to work your muscles and keep from getting faint, you must breathe deeply when you exercise. The shallow breathing that so many of us are accustomed to won't do. You have to inhale through your nose and fill your lungs as completely as possible with air. Shallow mouth breathing fills only your upper lung and if you rely on it you may find yourself feeling dizzy or faint or simply tired.

There are some instances where breathing can affect an exercise in a dramatic way. For example, if you inhale when you rise from a plié or rise up on your toes or begin a sideways bend, you'll lighten your upper body and achieve a better line and balance. Where breathing technique applies directly to a particular exercise, I've tried to make a note of it in the introduction to the exercise.

1   2   3

Spotting

Spotting is the term given to a technique that dancers use to keep themselves from getting dizzy when they turn. It's really a simple technique: Before a turn you focus on one particular spot. Your body turns while your head remains fixed, eyes looking at the "spot" until the very last minute, when the head turns in a 360-degree circle as quickly as possible until it's facing the "spot" once again. Your head is thus the last thing to turn. It's as if the body is spinning at 33 fluid RPM's while the head turns in staccato 45 RPM's. By focusing the eyes on one reference point and returning to that point immediately after a turn, you prevent dizziness because you keep yourself from seeing things slide by your eyes.

When dancers turn during a performance in a dark theater they must find some fixed point, often an "exit" sign or some other light that they can use for spotting. In a class or at home it's easier: You just pick out a picture on the wall, something outside the window, a book on a shelf, any immobile object that you can fix your eyes on.

You will be spotting in one of the exercises and in the dance routine, and you should practice the technique a few times before you try to use it. Stand holding your support and find something to "spot." Turn your body toward the support and continue turning until you're halfway around, keeping your eyes on your spot. Now snap your head in a complete circle, finding your spot in front of you, and follow the turn with your body until

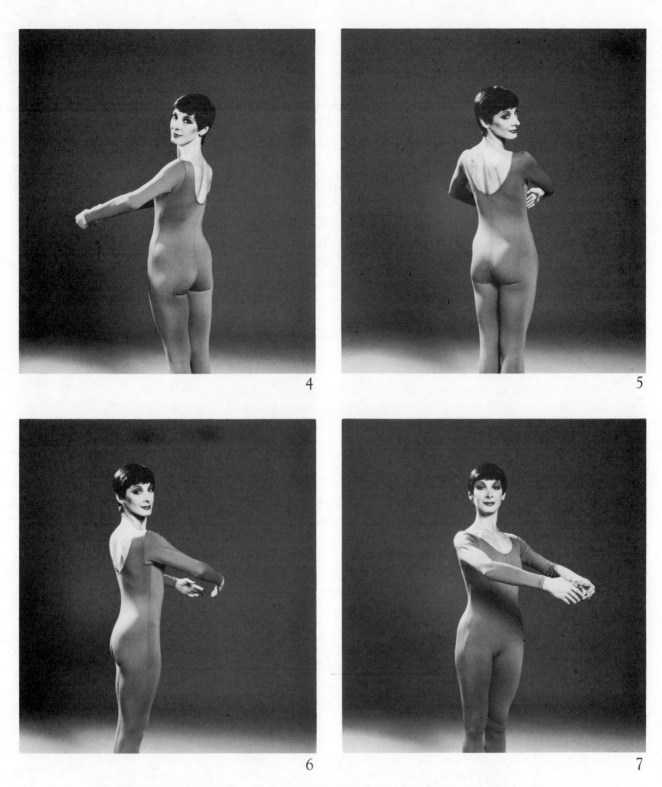

4

5

6

7

you're facing front again. There's no need to do these practice turns quickly; indeed it's better to try a few of them in slow motion until you get the hang of it. Remember to keep your head and neck relaxed. This is very important. Many people get into trouble with spotting because their necks are so stiff that they can't turn their heads freely.

Some Thoughts about the Floor

A teacher once told me something that I found quite helpful. She said to think about the floor not as a landing pad but as a springboard. Don't sink into a plié: make it almost seem that you are forcing your body down while it really wishes to lift into the air. When you reach out with your leg and your toe touches the floor, make it feel as though it wants to bounce upwards and would, if only you weren't holding it down. Imagine that you're dancing in a frying pan: the more time spent in the air, the better. Always work to create the look and feel of energy just barely restrained. That's what dance is all about.

Your Support

Ballet classes are routinely divided into two parts: work at the barre, followed by floor work. At the barre you work on the basics of form and technique, while on the floor you practice more complicated, performance-related steps. I've provided the same balance in this book. First there are the basic exercises, then the dance routine.

For the basic combinations you will need to use a support. In class, of course, we use a barre, but when I do these combinations at home I use a door frame or the back of a chair. The support is supposed to steady you but not bear your weight. Choose something that is stable and the correct height—midway between your waist and your shoulders. Anything from a bookshelf to a piano to the side of a bureau could be used. Just be sure it's not going to slide away from you in the middle of an exercise.

A Mirror?

You've no doubt noticed that one of the main features of a dance studio, in addition to the barre, is a mirror—sometimes many mirrors. A mirror is crucial to a professional dancer. There's just no other way to tell if your hips are straight and your arms held correctly. Though there are days when we all wish we could throw some sheets over the mirrors and just dance for fun, we know that we couldn't really do that—we're too concerned with getting it right.

You have to make peace with the mirror. It can be cruel, but it's also an essential method for correction and sometimes even encouragement. When we're on tour we sometimes have to take class on stage without mirrors. More than once I've felt that my dancing is terrible in these classes—my legs aren't as high as they should be, or my arms are awkward. But more often than not, when we reach the next town and can once again take class with a mirror, I find that the step that might feel unpolished in fact looks just fine when I see it myself. One of the most important functions of the mirror in dance is to bridge the gap between what a step feels like and what it looks like.

I think that it's very useful, but not essential, to have a mirror nearby when you exercise. In fact, it's more important in the very beginning when you're trying to get every step right and working on your posture and position. It helps enormously to be able, with the help of a mirror, to look at your posture from the side and to study how to lift your leg without lifting your hip and so on. You don't need to have a full-length mirror, though that's nice. You need only prop a mirror against the wall at an angle so it reflects your whole body. The image will be tilted, but you can still make corrections based on what you see.

Remember, if you do have a mirror, not to let it become too much of a crutch. Many dancers find that they become so obsessed with watching to get everything just right in the mirror that they lose a certain fluidity. If you're looking in the mirror constantly, you'll never be able to use your head and neck correctly. So be realistic about the mirror and don't let it get in the way.

Music

Music and tempo are important for ballet exercises. For one thing, music makes them more fun. Music is the soul of dance and there are some melodies that make you want to leap up and move. The music, in addition to being inspirational, dictates the speed and emphasis of an exercise. In fact, music not only helps you do an exercise correctly—at the proper speed and with the right emphasis—it also helps you remember an exercise. I remember dancing in the premiere of a ballet at the New York State Theater at Lincoln Center. I was in the midst of a pas de deux —the step was a lift—and my partner dropped me. Well, not quite dropped me. He held on to my ankle while my head brushed the floor. It wasn't his fault; the step was a particularly difficult one and the long skirt I was wearing made it hard for him to get a good grip on me. But there we were, trailing across the stage in a most awkward fashion. Ordinarily when this sort of thing happens you can regain your footing and recover. But this particular ballet was not choreographed to follow the music. You had to count carefully right from the beginning. If you lost count, you lost the ballet. We still had five more minutes of the pas de deux. My Hungarian partner, fiercely gripping my ankle, whispered, "Vat ve do now?" Knowing we couldn't recover the steps as learned, I commanded "Run . . . jeté . . . arabesque," and every other movement that seemed appropriate, and together we finished the dance. I had to bring the choreographer on stage for a bow after the ballet and I'm sure, after what had happened to his debut, he would have been happy to push me into the orchestra pit. But that's what can happen when you don't have the music as a constant underpinning to the dance.

By the same token, when it's time to rehearse a dance that I haven't done in years. I'm always convinced that I've forgotten the entire thing. But once I hear the music, all the steps come flooding back and it's as if I had just performed it the night before. Once you have music to accompany your exercises, it will be the same for you.

Rhythm refers to the beats in the music. A 2/4 beat would read 1, 2 / 1, 2 / 1, 2 / 1, 2, with the emphasis on the first count. A 4/4 beat would read 1, 2, 3, 4 / 1, 2, 3, 4 / 1, 2, 3, 4 / 1, 2, 3, 4, with the emphasis on the first beat.

If you don't know music, don't worry—there's no need to. For each exercise I've given not only the beat but also a familiar song in the correct beat that you can listen to as you exercise. Most of these exercises are counted in 4's or 8's. That's the way dancers count the music. It's easier to learn combinations of steps that way.

I think it's very helpful to have a tape of the correct music in the correct order that you can play as you exercise. If you have or can borrow a tape recorder, such a tape is simple to compile. If you don't care about a tape, simply hum the suggested songs to yourself so that you can feel the rhythm of the movements.

Dance Clothes

In a performance, a dancer must wear a prescribed costume. Most ballet costumes are beautiful, but there are certain ones that flatter certain bodies. For example, though I like to work in a tutu and fortunately have the proportions for one, some dancers don't. If your legs are too short or too long or your head too small, a tutu can emphasize your figure flaws. But a tutu will hide a hip problem and I'm always self-conscious about my hips. To me, a tutu or a chiffon skirt is the ideal costume, but unfortunately I can't always wear them. When it comes to class, of course, anything goes. You have only yourself to please. And it's the same for you when you do your ballet exercises. This is your opportunity to be frivolous and to indulge yourself! While you can exercise in anything from an old sweatshirt to your birthday suit, nothing will give you the kind of confidence and inspiration that real dance clothes can provide. After all, it's important to all of us to look good and to have our bodies look slim and graceful, because that's part of what dance is all about.

Dancers are very concerned about what they wear to a class and to the theater, sometimes to the point of becoming obsessed with a certain sweatshirt or pair of tights. Before a performance I always wear my "good luck" leg warmers and my "good luck" robe. Even though this particular robe is threadbare and ugly, I wear it before every performance while I put on my makeup. It has traveled all over the world with me. I also stand at the same barre when I warm up at the Met before a performance. If another dancer is already there, I ask him or her to move down. Fortunately we're all tolerant of one another's superstitions.

The best basic dance exercise outfit consists of tights, leotards and dance shoes. Fortunately there's a wide selection today of tights and leotards and you can pick any color or style that suits you.

All the women dancers I know, myself included, spend a great deal of time worrying about looking fat. So when we choose exercise clothes, we look for things that flatter our figures. Some dance teachers, especially those who teach children, prefer that their students wear pink or white tights and black or pink leotards: The light tights display the muscles of the legs distinctly, allowing a teacher to better correct the student's steps. But, as you probably know, dark tights are more flattering unless you have very slim legs. A leotard cut slightly high in the leg will also slenderize your legs and make them seem longer. The short chiffon ballet skirts that wrap and tie around your waist will hide and flatter your hips; you can find them in dance supply stores. A long T-shirt will have the same effect. And a low-cut top will help to lengthen a short neck.

To make yourself look as long and lean as possible, try to keep your clothes all in one color or in close shades of the same color. If you break up your line with two or three colors, you won't get the same beautiful effect.

We sometimes forget that dance clothes must do more than make us look good. They also have to keep us warm, so our muscles won't get cramped. When dancers begin a class we're all bundled up; gradually, as we stretch and warm up, off come the cover-ups. You should do the same.

I like to wear warm-up pants in a light stretch fabric. You can substitute sweatpants and they'll be just as effective, but some sweatpants are made of very heavy fabric and can make you look as if you have a snowsuit on. Leg warmers are also helpful in keeping your calves and ankles warm, and I like to arrange them so they go from mid-calf to just over the ankle. You might also want to add a top of some kind—a sweatshirt or T-shirt or some type of vest—over your leotard to keep your chest warm until you've gotten into your routine.

Hair

My hair is short now after years of being long, and I love the simplicity of it. In American Ballet Theatre I can get away with short hair because we often wear headpieces during performances. In the Royal Ballet of London many of the dancers have short hair and they wear beautifully constructed wigs. Of course, the most common ballet look is the one adopted by the dancers at the New York City Ballet, who all have long hair worn in high buns.

If you have long hair, you don't want it to get in your way as you dance. Tie it back in a ponytail or a braid of some kind. You can wear a headband, but if your hair is very long a headband won't keep it under control when you turn or bend over.

Dance Shoes

You can be frivolous about your exercise clothes, but you should take your shoes seriously. You don't have to go out and buy anything fancy— you can even exercise in your bare feet—but if you do buy exercise shoes they must be well fitted and of the correct type.

I don't recommend doing ballet exercises in sneakers because they won't allow you to point your foot or work your foot on the floor properly. The best shoes to wear are traditional ballet shoes. You can buy these shoes—they're soft and come in pink, white or black—at any dance supply store. Buy the kind with the soft leather sole. It's best to choose ballet shoes that bend easily in your hand. Usually you can depend on a salesperson to help you with the fit. Correct fit is absolutely crucial. The shoes will seem too tight at first if you've never worn a pair. That's because they must fit the foot absolutely snugly. In fact, you may find you wear a ballet shoe a size or two smaller than your street shoe size. But be sure that your toes aren't curled up inside the shoe. And, by the way, there's no left or right shoe when you buy them; as you wear them they'll mold to your feet and become either left or right.

You'll have to sew on the elastic that comes with the shoes yourself. To find exactly where they should be sewn, fold the shoe inwards in half so that the heel is pressed against the toe. Right in front of the fold is where you should sew your elastics.

All dancers break in their shoes before wearing them, and you might want to do so too. You simply work the shoes in your hands, twisting them and kneading them so that they're as soft and supple as they can be before you put them on. Sometimes a little rubbing alcohol rubbed on the outside of the shoe when your foot is in it will mold it to your foot more quickly.

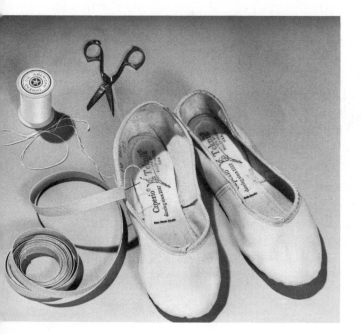

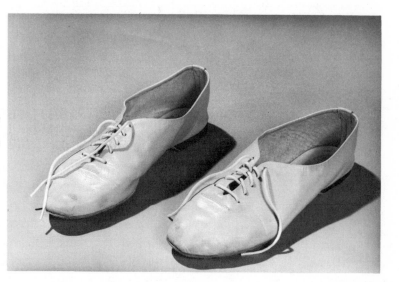

How to Use This Book

This book has fourteen exercises that warm you up, stretch you and strengthen you, and one dance routine. You can do them in any order and combination that you like, though I think it's best to do the exercises together with the dance routine when you have time and just the exercises alone when you don't. I don't recommend doing the dance routine alone unless your body is already warmed up—either with a few of the ballet exercises or some other form of exercise. I once pulled a muscle in my calf because I wasn't warmed up when I attempted a difficult jumping step. It seems to take forever to recover from such an injury and it's uncomfortable and easily prevented.

The exercises should take about thirty to forty-five minutes to do once you're familiar with them. But you have to allow yourself a few run-throughs before you can expect the exercises to really benefit your body. The first few times you do them you'll be working for accuracy. It's very important that you do each exercise precisely as described. Those first few times won't really be working your muscles fully or getting you into a sweat, but that's not what's important in the beginning. After you've done them a few times your body will "know" them, and you can work for fluidity and speed up a bit or slow down, according to the tempo of the exercise. Some of the slow ones should slow down more as you become more proficient, while the fast ones can get faster for maximum benefit.

The movements are deceptively simple—when you first study them you may not think they're strenuous enough. But believe me, once you know them and can move through all of them without stopping, you'll find they'll give you a terrific workout.

I suggest that you do the exercises and/or the dance routine about three times a week. It can be beneficial to skip a day in between because it gives your muscles a chance to recover. However, as times goes by and you get more flexible and in better condition, you may find that exercising almost every day is just right for you.

Personally, I hate to exercise but, like all dancers, I find that after a few days of inactivity I'm quickly out of shape. When that happens, I can actually see a muscle twitch when I lift a leg and there's no strength in that leg. That's why I developed these exercises in the first place—so I can keep limber when I can't get to a class. And of course I always find that once I've begun the exercises and the blood gets circulating I start to feel good, and by the time I'm finished I feel completely revitalized and invigorated. I hope you find them as useful and effective as I do!

PART TWO

The Exercises

Exercise 1

This is a simple routine that I always do just before class while standing at the barre. It's a beginning stretch that limbers your neck, legs and shoulders while it gets your blood circulating.

Remember that while you do this routine, you should be constantly exerting a certain amount of pressure against your support, whether it's a barre or a doorjamb. When you do any kind of ballet exercises, you should imagine that every movement you make is being made against resistance. Don't ever let momentum carry you; always control your movements.

The count of the exercise should follow the beat of the suggested music. **Each numbered step in the exercises that follow represents one beat.**

Tempo: adagio, slow 4/4, as in "The Way We Were."

Starting Position: Stand about a foot away from the support, facing it, both arms grasping support, feet parallel, a few inches apart.

Achilles Stretch

1. Bend your left knee as you slide your right foot back about 6 inches. Keep your weight on the left foot and press slightly against the support as your foot goes back. You'll feel a slight pressure in your right calf and Achilles tendon.

2. Now trying to keep both feet flat on the floor, bend your right knee slightly. You'll feel the stretch in the front of your right leg and also in your calf and Achilles tendon.

3. Straighten your right knee as you press against your support.

4. Bring your right foot forward and back to the original position.

- Repeat movement with left leg to a count of 4.
- Repeat movement with right leg to a count of 4.
- Repeat movement with left leg to a count of 4.

Shoulder Rolls

1. Roll shoulders forward and then up.

2. Roll shoulders back and down.

3, 4. Repeat backward roll.

5. Roll shoulders back and then up.

6. Roll shoulders forward and down.

7, 8. Repeat forward roll.

1. Tilt your head to the right side, feeling the stretch along the left side of your neck. Don't let your head just drop and don't force your head down; stay in control of the stretch.

2. Return to center.

3. Tilt your head to the left side.

4. Return to center.

5. Look down, feeling the pull in the back of your neck. Don't let your head just fall; stay in control.

6. Return to center.

7. Look straight up to the ceiling, feeling the stretch in your throat. Keep your shoulders down and your mouth closed. (If you open your mouth, you'll feel a strain in the back of your neck.) Do not try to look behind you (again, doing so could strain your neck); look straight up.

8. Return to center.

● There are 32 counts in Exercise 1. You can repeat the whole exercise from the beginning for a total of 64 counts.

Exercise 2

Most of the exercises are done with the feet at right angles to each other, heels about an inch apart. Trained dancers will turn their feet out more than this, but it's a mistake to try an exaggerated "turnout" if you're untrained because you can pull a muscle and, in fact, you won't be working the correct muscles.

This exercise stretches your Achilles tendon. If, when you plié, you simply lower your body and raise it, you won't feel much, but you'll feel the exercise in the whole leg and into the thigh if you're giving good resistance. If you've never tried a plié before, see pages 24–25 for a description of how it should be done.

Tempo: 6/8 time, as in "Amazing Grace."

Starting Position: Holding the support with your left hand, stand with your heels an inch or so apart, toes turned out only as far as is comfortable. Your right arm is relaxed at your side.

1, 2. Bend both knees and lower your body to the floor as far as you can while still keeping your heels down. As you lower your body, lift your right arm almost to shoulder height.

3, 4. Straightening your knees, lower your right arm to your side (starting position).

• Repeat plié to a count of 4.

3, 4. Lift arm up above your head, looking at your hand, keeping your wrist graceful.

1, 2. Bring right arm forward to shoulder height.

5, 6. Bring arm back behind your body in a large circle.

7, 8. Bring arm down to your side to the starting position, still watching the hand.

● Repeat two pliés, 4 counts each, for a total of 8 counts, then . . .

1, 2. In a reverse circle, raise your right arm back behind your body.

3, 4. Stretch it all the way back, then

5, 6. up and over your head,

7, 8. and then forward and down to original position at side.

Move right foot about 12 inches from left foot, feet still turned out as far as is comfortable.

1, 2. Bend both knees and lower your torso as far as you can, keeping your heels on the floor, as you lift your right arm. (You'll be able to go lower in this plié than in the first because your feet are farther apart.)

3, 4. Straightening your knees, lift your torso to starting position, lowering your right arm to your side.

5, 6, 7, 8. Repeat plié and return to starting position.

1, 2. Watching your right hand, raise your right arm to just below shoulder height and reach to the right as far as you can, feeling the stretch in the right arm and the left side.

3, 4. Lower your arm to starting position.

5, 6, 7, 8. Repeat arm stretch and lower arm to starting position.

● Keeping your right foot about 12 inches from left foot, feet still turned out as far as is comfortable, repeat two pliés for 4 counts each and two arm stretches to the right for 4 counts each.

Now turn and repeat entire exercise, holding the support with your right hand.

Exercise 3

This is a deceptively simple stretch because it sounds and looks easy, but in fact it's a wonderful warm-up and by the time you finish it you should have worked up a good glow. I often do this exercise holding on to a door frame.

Remember that, when you are pointing your foot to the front, the side and then back, if you just stick your toe out, you won't be really getting the benefits of the balletic movement. You must move your foot as if you're pushing against a weight, feeling the muscles working in the entire leg.

In this exercise we repeat a movement in a typical ballet pattern: to the front, to the side, to the back, and then a break, and then in reverse to the back, side and front, and then another break. If you pay attention to this pattern, you'll find that an exercise that at first might seem complicated is in fact quite simple. It's understanding these patterns that allows dancers to learn and remember steps quickly. Look for these patterns as you work your way through the exercises.

Tempo: 3/4 time, as in "Try to Remember" from *The Fantasticks*. This is a waltz tempo with a strong emphasis on the first beat. The numbers in parentheses—(2,3)—simply mean that you hold a position through the two extra beats in each waltz measure. This will seem very natural when you exercise to waltz music.

Starting Position: Hold support with left hand, toes turned out as far as is comfortable, heels together, right arm relaxed at side.

46

1. (2,3) From the starting position, raise your right arm slowly in front of you, leading with your wrist. As you raise your arm, bend forward from the hips without bending your waist. Stop the movement when your hand is on a level with your head.

2. (2,3) Return to starting position.

3. (2,3) Brush your right foot forward until your foot is pointed in front of you, your toe on the floor. As you move your foot, lift your right arm to the side until it's just below shoulder height.

4. (2,3) Return to starting position.

● Repeat to count of 4, but on the third count brush your right foot, toe pointed, **to the side.**

● Repeat to count of 4, but on the third count brush your right foot, toe pointed, **to the rear.**

1. (2,3) Keeping your heels together and touching the floor, plié until your knees are directly over your toes. You'll feel the stretch in your inner thighs and calves. Lift your right arm slightly as you lower your torso.

2. (2,3) Straightening your knees, return to starting position, lowering your arm.

3. (2,3) Rise onto the balls of your feet, slightly lifting your right arm as you go up.

4. (2,3) Return to starting position.

To a count of 8:
From the starting position, bend your knees as far as you can bend with feet flat on floor and crouch forward until your head is hanging in front of your shins. Your neck and shoulders are completely relaxed, hand resting on the floor in front of you. . . .

. . . Keeping your torso relaxed, straighten your knees so you're bent in half, hand still touching the floor (if you can).

Begin to roll your torso up, slowly uncurling upward, until you're completely upright.

To another count of 8:
Lift your right arm out to the side.

Watching your right hand, lift the arm up in an arc, bending at the waist until you are stretched to the side toward your support, with your right (working) arm reaching toward your left (supporting) hand.

● Repeat the entire sequence (32 counts) from the beginning.

Then turn, hold support with your right hand and do the whole sequence twice with the left arm and leg.

Exercise 4

In this exercise you will be changing weight from foot to foot, from side to side. As you make these shifts you must concentrate on using your thigh and calf muscles to get from one foot to the other; if you're simply bouncing from toe to toe, you won't feel the effect of the exercise. A tip on breathing is to inhale when you're shifting your weight from one foot to the other because your body is lighter when the lungs are full and your working leg will be better able to make the weight shift. You might also try to remember to inhale when rising from a plié. The movement of the arms should be smooth. They'll swing in an arc to the front, then down and then to the side and finally down as you shift your weight. Let your arms be free and graceful as your legs do the work.

Tempo: 2/4 time, as in "Singing in the Rain."

Starting Position: Left hand holding your support, heels together, feet turned out as far as is comfortable.

Starting front:

1. Lift right hand in front of you to shoulder height and, as you're lifting your hand, point your right foot and extend it in front of you, keeping your right toe on the floor.

2. Pushing from your left foot, shift your weight to your right foot as you lower your right arm to your side.

3. As your weight shifts, point your left toe behind you and lower your right heel to the floor, swinging your right arm out to the side to just above shoulder height.

4. Shift weight back to the left heel, again lowering your right arm.

5. Point the right toe again, as your arm is lifted up in front of you to shoulder height.

6. Bring your right heel back next to the left heel so that feet are in the starting position and your right arm is lowered to the side.

7. Go up on the balls of your feet, right arm lifting slightly to the side.

8. Bending your knees, lower your body into a plié until your knees are over your toes. Your heels stay on the floor.

Now side shifts with plié:

1. Lift your torso, straightening your knees, and as you lift point your right foot to the side. Lift your right arm to just above shoulder height.

3. Rise from plié, pointing the left toe on the floor and lifting both arms overhead.

2. Lower into a plié with feet about 12 inches apart.

4. Bring left heel in to meet right heel.

5. Point left toe out to side, keeping it on the floor.

6. Lower into plié, letting left heel come to the floor. Arms are lowered and joined in a circle in front of thighs.

7. Extend arms out to side as you straighten left leg and grab support with left hand. Your weight is supported on your left foot, right toe pointed to side and on the floor. ▶

8. Bring right heel in to join left. Your right arm is relaxed at side in starting position.

Now starting back:

1. Extend right leg back, toe pointed, as right arm extends forward at just below shoulder height. ▼

2. Shift weight back to right foot as arm comes down to side.

3. Point left toe in front of you, lifting your right arm to just below shoulder height at the side.

4. Shift your weight to the left foot and as your left heel comes down, bring your arm down.

5. Point your right toe behind you again, lifting your right arm to the side to just below shoulder height.

6. As you bring your right heel forward to join the left in the starting position, lower your arm.

7. Go up on the balls of your feet, right arm extended to side.

8. Lower into plié, keeping your heels on the floor and lowering your arm.

- Repeat side shifts with plié (starts on page 54) for a total of 8 counts.

Repeat entire sequence on other side, holding support with right hand.

Exercise 5

This exercise is a series of knee pick-ups followed by foot and knee flexes and a full forward bend. It develops flexibility in your hips, which is important for graceful movement. It will also stretch your thighs.

Be sure that as you flex your feet, you feel resistance. Don't just bring the foot in; instead feel the knee pull out as the foot comes in. That's the only way you'll really get the right tension in the leg muscles.

In this exercise, once again, we repeat a movement in a typical ballet pattern: to the front, to the side, to the back, and then a break, followed by the same movement but this time to the back, the side, the front, and another break.

Tempo: 2/4, as in "Tea for Two."

1, 2. Lift your right leg, bending your right knee. At the same time, grasp your right knee with your right hand to help pull the knee to your chest. You'll feel the stretch in your left as well as your right thigh.

3, 4. Releasing your hold, lower your right knee, straightening the leg until your foot and arm are in the starting position.

Starting Position: Left hand holding your support, heels together, feet turned out as far as is comfortable.

5. Point your right toe and lift the right leg straight in front of you until the foot is about 12 inches from the floor. As you're lifting the foot, raise your right arm gracefully in front of you until it's above your head.

6. Bend your right knee and flex your right foot, bringing the foot about 6 inches toward your left leg. Your arm remains above your head.

7. Point the right foot, straightening the knee until the leg is straight in front of you, foot pointing, about 12 inches above the floor.

8. Return right foot to starting position as you lower your right arm to your side.

● Repeat first 4 counts (knee pick-up), then . . .

5. Point your right toe and lift your right leg to the side until the foot is about 12 inches from the floor. As you're lifting the foot, raise your right arm gracefully in front of you until it's above your head.

6. Bend your right knee and flex your right foot, bringing the foot about 6 inches toward your left leg. Your arm remains above your head.

7. Point the right foot, straightening the knee until the leg is stretched out to the side, foot pointing, about 12 inches above the floor.

8. Return right foot to starting position as you lower your right arm to your side.

● Repeat first 4 counts (knee pick-up), then . . .

5. Point your right toe and lift the right leg behind you until the foot is about 12 inches from the floor. As you're lifting the foot, raise your right arm gracefully in front of you until it's above your head.

6. Bend your right knee and flex your right foot, bringing the foot about 6 inches toward your left leg. Your knee will be turned out slightly to the side as you do this in order to work the right muscles. Your arm remains above your head.

7. Point the right foot, straightening the knee until the leg is stretched out directly behind you about 12 inches above the floor.

8. Return right foot to starting position, but keep your right arm extended over your head.

1, 2, 3, 4. Looking up at your hand, bend forward from the waist, bringing your arm with you as you descend. Stretch forward until your torso is parallel to the floor, then continue bending forward, keeping your back as straight as possible until your hand is touching the floor and your head and neck are relaxed and hanging down. You should feel a good stretch in the back of your legs.

5, 6, 7, 8. Lifting your arm and then following with your head and shoulders, unbend from the waist until you are completely upright. Lower your arm to your side.

● Now we repeat the whole sequence again from the beginning, but this time starting to the back, then pointing to the side, and finally to the front:

To a count of 4, pick up your right knee and lower it, as in the first movement of 4 counts, then . . .

To a count of 4, do a point, flex, point **behind** you with your right leg.

To a count of 4, pick up your right knee and lower it as in the first movement, then . . .

To a count of 4, do a point, flex, point **to the right side** with your right leg.

To a count of 4, pick up your right knee and lower it as in the first movement, then . . .

To a count of 4, do a point, flex, point **in front** of you with your right leg. After your feet return to the starting position, keep your right arm poised above your head.

1, 2, 3, 4. Looking up at your hand, bend forward from the waist, bringing your arm with you as you descend, stretching forward until your torso is parallel to the floor. Continue bending forward, keeping your back as straight as possible, until your hand is touching the floor and your head and neck are relaxed and hanging down. You should feel a good stretch in the back of your legs.

waist until you are completely upright. Lower your arm to your side.

5, 6, 7, 8. Lifting your arm and then following with your head and shoulders, unbend from the

Repeat the entire exercise, holding your support with your right arm and working the left leg and arm.

Exercise 6

This exercise is for the strength and flexibility of the foot and the leg. It also works the inner thigh.

One of the important movements of this exercise is the "brush," where you extend your foot by brushing it along the floor away from the body, then releasing it up off the floor. There's a technique to this movement that's important. If you simply push your foot forward, for example, you won't be working your leg properly. Instead you must try to lead with the heel, when the foot is brushing forward, or the toe, when the foot is brushing to the rear. It might sound like an insignificant detail, but if you try the movement, first moving your foot forward while leading with your toe and then moving your foot forward while leading with the heel, you'll feel and see the difference in the muscles used. When you return the foot to the starting position, you must reverse the movement and lead with the toe (returning from a forward brush) or the heel (returning from a brush to the back).

Tempo: 4/4 time, as in a Sousa march like "Stars and Stripes."

Starting Position: Left hand holding your support, heels together, feet turned out as far as is comfortable.

1. Keeping your knee straight, brush your foot forward, leading with the heel and pointing the toe, until your foot, with toe pointed, is about 12 inches off the floor. Your foot should be turned out as much as is comfortable when the leg is fully extended.

64

2. Now leading with the toe, bring the foot back to the starting position.

3. Repeat forward brush.

4. Repeat return.

5. Repeat forward brush.

6. Bend your right knee and bring your pointed toe in to just touch the front of your supporting ankle, turning your right knee out to the side as you bring your foot in. ▶

7. Straighten bent knee and bring right leg forward again with toe pointed so that the foot is about 12 inches from the floor.

8. Return foot to starting position.

● Repeat first 8 counts, but this time work your leg **to the right side.**

● Then repeat first 8 counts but this time work your leg **to your rear,** being careful not to "sickle" or curl your foot when you bring it in to touch the back of your supporting ankle (you should feel the stretch in the inner thigh). Then . . .

Remember not to move any other part of your body as you swing your leg forward and back in these movements.

1. Keeping your torso and your knees straight, swing your leg forward, pointing your toe as you lift your foot about 12 inches from the floor.

2. Swing your leg directly behind you, trying to lead with the toe. The foot passes through the starting position, where the heels briefly meet, before continuing the swing to the rear. Point the toe as the leg swings to the rear until the foot is about a foot from the floor.

3, 4. Repeat leg swings, forward and back.

5, 6. Repeat again.

7. Swing leg forward.

8. Return to starting position.

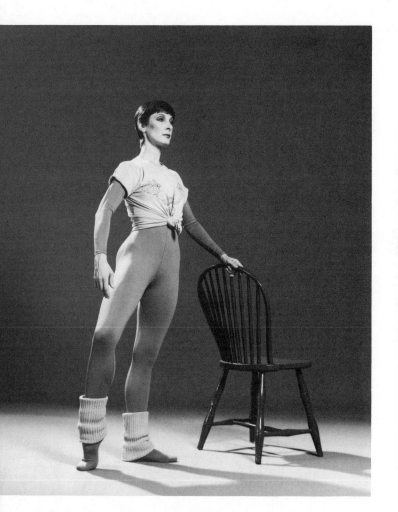

1. Rolling your foot as you lift it from the floor —it should go about 3 inches off the floor—lift the right knee to the side, pointing the toe as the knee goes up.

2. Roll the foot back into the starting position.

3,4, 5,6, 7,8. Repeat three more foot lifts.

1. Pointing your toe, brush your right foot to the side and lift it about 12 inches from the floor.

2. Lower your foot to the floor as you shift your weight so you're supported by both legs. Holding your torso straight, bend your knees into a plié, keeping your heels on the floor. Lift your right arm slightly as your torso is lowered.

3. Straightening your knees, raise your torso and, when your legs are straight, rise onto the balls of your feet.

4. Lower into plié again.

5. Rise from plié onto the balls of your feet.

6. Lower into plié again.

7. Rise from plié again, both feet flat on floor, and shift your weight back onto your left foot, right foot extended to the side with pointed toe about a foot off the floor.

8. Return right leg to starting position.

1. Rolling your foot as you lift it from the floor, lift the right knee to the side, pointing the toe as the knee goes up.

2. Roll the foot back into the starting position.

3,4, 5,6, 7,8. Repeat three more foot lifts.

● Repeat the entire exercise from the beginning, but this time reverse the pattern so in the first movement you brush your foot **to the rear,** then to **the side,** and then **to the front.**

Repeat entire exercise to the other side, working the left leg.

Exercise 7

This exercise consists of foot brushes like the ones you've done previously. It also includes a movement that's good for hip flexibility—making a half circle on the floor with your foot. As I mentioned before, this half-circle movement, called a rond de jambe, is the one my Los Angeles teacher describes as pulling an oar through the water. That image will help you keep the right feeling in the leg. And finally you'll be doing a few side bends that will help to stretch out your arms and limber your waist.

Tempo: 3/4 time, as in "My Favorite Things" from *The Sound of Music.*

Starting Position: Holding the support with your left hand, stand with your heels an inch or so apart, toes turned out only as far as is comfortable. Your right arm is relaxed at your side.

1. Brush your right foot forward, pointing your toe, until the foot is about 12 inches from the floor. As you raise your foot, lift your arm forward to just below shoulder height.

70

2. Lower your toe to the floor and lean forward slightly, bending your right knee. Your foot will be turned out as far as is comfortable. Then roll your foot down until it's flat on the floor and shift your weight forward onto the right foot.

3. Pushing against the floor with your right foot, shift your weight back to the left foot, pointing your right toe while keeping it on the floor, and bending your left knee.

4. Keeping your right toe on the floor, make a half circle with your foot, until it is extended behind you, toe still pointed. Bring your right arm to the side as the foot moves to the side, leaving the arm extended at just below shoulder height while the leg continues its half circle to the rear.

5. Bring both the right arm and leg back to the front, passing through the starting position, until they're both extended forward, toe still pointed, right foot lifted about 12 inches from the floor. The left knee straightens as the right leg passes through the starting position.

7. Pushing off the floor with your right foot, shift your weight back to the left foot—left knee stays straight this time—pointing your right toe and kicking your right foot up so it's about 12 inches off the floor.

8. Bring your right foot and right arm back into the starting position.

6. Roll your right foot down onto the floor until it's flat, bending your right knee and shifting your weight forward onto the right foot. Your right arm will remain extended in front of you at just below shoulder height.

This side bend to the left and then to the right should take a total of 8 counts. Do it in a single smooth motion.

1, 2, 3, 4. Brush your right leg to the side (keep your pointed toe on the floor) as you lift your right arm to the side to just below shoulder height. Continue lifting your right arm until it is over your head. Keeping your hips level (don't lift your right hip!), bend at the waist to the left, leading with your arm until you're stretched over to the side and your right arm is almost

touching your left hand on the support. Begin unbending, lifting your right arm until it's just over your head. Keep unbending until your torso is upright, and lower your right arm to just below shoulder height. Release your support and extend both arms to the side as you lower your heel to the floor. Your feet will be about 12 inches apart, weight distributed evenly.

5, 6, 7, 8. Shifting your weight to your right foot, point your left toe, and put your right hand on your right hip, your left arm over your head. Do side bend to the right side. Come back up straight through wide position again, both feet flat on the floor, and shift weight to left foot, pointing right toe to side. Return to starting position.

Now repeat the first 8 counts in reverse, this time starting to the back:

2. Lower your toe to the floor and lean backward slightly, bending your right knee. Then roll your foot down until it's flat on the floor and shift your weight backward to the right leg.

1. Brush your right foot to the rear, pointing your toe, until the foot is about 12 inches from the floor. As you raise your foot, lift your arm in front of you to just below shoulder height.

3. Pushing off the floor with your right foot, shift your weight back to the left foot, pointing your right toe behind you, bending your left knee.

4. Keeping your right toe on the floor, make a half circle with your leg until your foot, toe still pointed, is extended in front of you. Extend your right arm to your side as your right foot moves to the side, leaving the arm extended at just below shoulder height while the leg continues its half circle to the front.

5. Straighten your left leg as you brush back with your right foot, moving your arm and leg through the starting position, until your right leg is extended about 12 inches from the floor, toe still pointed. Your right arm extends forward.

6. Roll your right foot down on to the floor until it's flat, leaning backward slightly, bending your right knee, and shifting your weight back to the right foot. Your right arm will remain extended in front of you at just below shoulder height.

7. Pushing off the floor with your right foot, shift your weight forward to the left foot—left knee stays straight this time—pointing your right toe and lifting your right foot to the rear so it's about 12 inches off the floor.

8. Bring your right foot and right arm back to the starting position.

- **To a count of 4,** repeat the side bend to the left (pages 74–75), and then . . .
- **To a count of 4,** repeat the side bend to the right (page 76), finishing in the starting position.

Repeat entire exercise, holding the support with your right hand.

80

Exercise 8

This exercise consists of a body curl and foot extensions. The body curl helps develop grace and balance, and it gently stretches your back muscles. The foot extensions are very good for the inner thigh as well as the outer thigh. They also help to loosen the hip joint.

As you curl your body in toward the support, remember to let out your breath and release all the tension from your body. Let everything drop. Then, when you're ready to come up and extend your leg, inhale and pull everything up and together. It's the letting go and then pulling together that creates the useful work of this exercise. It's relax and tense; relax and tense.

Tempo: 2/4 time, as in "The Girl from Ipanema."

1. Curl your body toward your support this way: Bend your left knee and lead your body into a curl by bringing your right arm around in front of you. Curl your head and torso down and to the left. Simultaneously bending your right knee as you lift your right foot with toe pointed, bring your toe to rest on the inside of the left ankle.

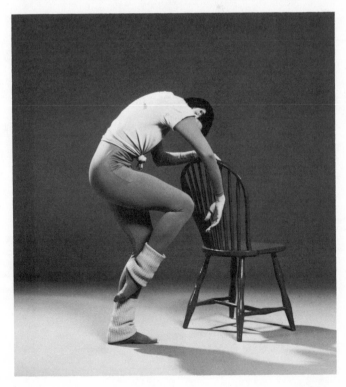

Starting Position: Holding the support with your left hand, stand with your heels an inch or so apart, toes turned out only as far as is comfortable. Your right arm is relaxed at your side.

2. Uncurl your body, straightening both knees, and extend your right foot forward about 12 inches off the floor with toe pointed and turned out as far as you can. As you uncurl, extend your arm to the side. You should feel the stretch in your thigh.

3. Lower your pointed right toe to the floor.

4. Brush your foot back to the starting position, leading with the toe as you lower your arm to the starting position.

• Repeat this movement to a count of 4.

● Repeat the entire first movement twice to a count of 8—two forward curls with leg extensions for 4 counts each—but point your foot **to the rear** this time.

● Repeat the entire first movement twice to a count of 8—two forward curls with leg extensions for 4 counts each—but point your foot **to the side** instead of to the front.

1, 2. Curl your body, straight forward this time, by bending both knees, pointing and lifting your left foot until it's resting at the side of your right knee, bending your head down as far as you can toward your knee and extending your right arm past your head, which is forward and down.

3, 4. Uncurl your body, straightening both knees, and return to starting position.

5, 6. Rise onto the balls of your feet and, keeping your shoulders down, stretch your right arm to the side and diagonally up into the air. Keep looking at your hand as you move your arm above your head. Feel the stretch all along your right side.

7, 8. Lower your arm to your side and roll your feet back onto the floor until you're back to the starting position.

● Repeat the entire exercise in reverse pattern, but this time instead of lowering your pointed toe to the floor on the count of 3, **hold your leg off the floor** for an extra count to build strength. The first points will be to the rear:

Curl toward your support and point **to the rear** twice, each to a count of 4.

Curl toward your support and point **to the side** twice, each to a count of 4.

Curl toward your support and point **to the front** twice, each to a count of 4.

Now curl forward, uncurl, rise onto balls of feet, and lower, to a count of 8, just as you did the first time.

Repeat the entire exercise, holding the support with your right hand.

85

Exercise 9

This is a series of high leg-raises and kicks. It's an exercise that will warm you up quickly and get your blood pumping. When you raise your legs you'll be doing it slowly, trying to maintain control of the thigh muscles. The kicks, on the other hand, are done quickly and with zest.

Kicking the leg is quite an easy movement with a simple technique: The leg is free going up and controlled going down. Whenever a line of dancers—the Rockettes come to mind of course—kick in unison, they thrill the audience. The unity of movement is impressive, but in fact the step is fun and fairly simple. The kicks, which are known as grand battements (*battement* from "beating"), should be done with as much vigor as possible. You'll want your leg lifted up high in the air. If you think of the floor as being as hot as a griddle, it will help give the idea of how your legs should bounce into the air away from the heat. Your torso remains straight throughout the lifts and kicks except for those to the back, where you can shift your torso very slightly forward. Remember not to raise the hip of the leg that's being lifted and not to raise the heel of the standing leg off the floor. Remember also to keep your standing leg straight as you kick the other leg; don't yield to the temptation to bend the standing knee to get the kicking leg higher. And finally, after you kick the leg up don't let it just fall down; try to control it as it returns to the starting position. You'll get so much more out of the exercise if you control the descent.

On this exercise you have a sort of "and" count between counts 3 and 4 in the first sequence. Because it's a waltz tempo, it gives the chance to get one little extra movement in there, and of course we take advantage of this. So the count goes: 1 (2, 3), 2 (2, 3), 3 (2, *and*) 4 (2, 3). Even though there are four counts, using that "and" we get five movements.

Tempo: 3/4 (waltz) time, as in "Moon River."

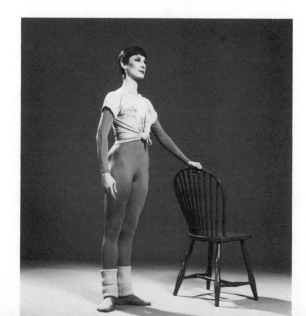

Starting Position: Holding the support with your left, hand, stand with your heels an inch or so apart, toes turned out only as far as is comfortable. Your right arm is relaxed at your side.

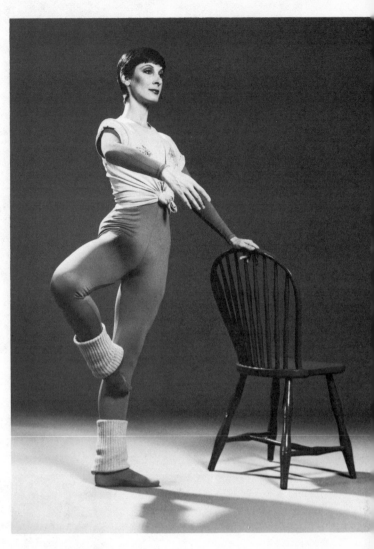

2. (2, 3) Bend your right knee as you straighten the left and, bringing the knee out to the right side, place your right foot just below the inside of your left knee. Keep the right knee turned out to the side.

1. (2, 3) Extend your right leg, toe pointed, in front of you, lifting it as high as you can while you bend your left knee without lifting your left heel off the floor. While you're doing this, extend your right arm in front of you to just below shoulder height.

3. (2) Straighten the right leg and point the toe, touching the floor in front of you. ◄
(and) Kick the right leg up into the air in front of you as high as you can. ▼

4. (2, 3) Trying to lead with the toe, bring the foot and arm down to the starting position.

1. (2, 3) Extend your right leg, toe pointed, to the side, lifting it as high as you can while you bend your left knee without lifting your left heel off the floor. While you're doing this, extend your right arm to your side to just below shoulder height.

2. (2, 3) Bend your right knee as you straighten the left and, keeping the knee out to the right side, bring your right foot in to just below the inside of your left knee.

3. (2) Straighten the right leg and point the toe, touching the floor directly to the side. ◀
(and) Kick the right leg up into the air to your side as high as you can. ▼

4. (2, 3) Trying to lead with the heel, bring the foot and arm down to the starting position.

2. (2, 3) Bend your right knee as you straighten the left and, bringing the knee out to the right side, place your right foot just below the inside of your left knee. Keep the right knee turned out to the side.

1. (2, 3) Extend your right leg, toe pointed, behind you, lifting it as high as you can while keeping your torso as straight as possible. At the same time, bend your left knee without lifting your left heel off the floor. While you're doing this, extend your right arm in front of you at just below shoulder height.

3. (2) Straighten the right leg and point the toe, touching the floor directly behind you. ▶

(and) Kick the right leg up into the air behind you as high as you can, while keeping your back straight. ▼

4. (2, 3) Trying to lead with the heel, bring the foot and arm down to the starting position.

2. Lifting your arm over your head as you watch your hand, begin to stretch backward, pulling up from the waist and never losing control of the lower back. When you're completely stretched, your arm will be past your head and slightly to the right side.

3. Gradually bring your arm back so that it's in front of you, while you straighten your back.

4. Return your arm to the starting position and bring your foot back to the starting position by brushing in and leading with the toe.

1. Brush your right foot in front of you with toe pointed, keeping the toe on the floor while you extend your right arm to the front.

• Repeat everything except the last 4 counts in reverse pattern, kicking your leg first **to the rear,** then **to the side,** then **to the front.**

(*continued*)

Then repeat the last 4 counts just as you did them the first time:

1. Brush your right foot behind you with toe pointed, keeping the toe on the floor while you extend your right arm to the front.

2. Lifting your arm over your head as you watch your hand, begin to stretch backward, pulling up from the waist and never losing control of the lower back. When you're completely stretched, your arm will be past your head and slightly to the right side.

3. Gradually bring your arm back so that it's in front of you, while you bring your back upright.

4. Return your arm to the starting position and bring your foot back to the starting position by brushing in and leading with the heel.

Repeat the entire exercise to the other side, holding your support with your right hand.

Exercise 10

This exercise consists of bent leg raises, high leg extensions and full body stretches to the side. It's an excellent exercise for strengthening the legs, abdomen and back. It's very important to remember that when you do the leg raises, both the bent leg ones and the high ones, you must keep your hips level. Don't let the hip on the working side lift, though you may feel the impulse to let it do so. Even though it prevents your getting your leg up high, it's important to keep your hips level so you work the right muscles. Just get the legs as high as you can while keeping the right line.

Tempo: 3/4 slow waltz time, for example "Edelweiss" from *The Sound of Music*. By the way, the more slowly you do this exercise, the more difficult it becomes, so start out by doing it to a slightly fast waltz time and, as you become more proficient, you can slow down the pace.

Starting Position: Holding the support with your left hand, stand with your heels an inch or so apart, toes turned out only as far as is comfortable. Your right arm is relaxed at your side.

1. Lift your right arm to the side and continue lifting it in an arc over your head, as you bend your head and torso until your right hand is almost touching your support on the left. You'll feel the stretch all along your right side. At the same time, lift your right leg, knee bent, in front of you, thigh parallel to the floor or higher.

2. Straighten your torso, bringing your arm back in an arc until it's extended to the side.

3. Straighten your right leg and lift it to the front as high as you can, stretching it upward and feeling the muscles in the back of the thigh. Don't straighten the knee with a snap; straighten it with control, lifting it as you straighten. Be sure to keep your hips level.

4. Bring your arm back to the starting position as you swing your leg down, brushing your foot back to the starting position.

- Repeat the entire movement to a count of 4, this time lifting your leg **to the side.**

98

● Repeat the entire movement to a count of 4, this time lifting your leg **to the rear.**

From the starting position, release your support and lower both arms to your sides.

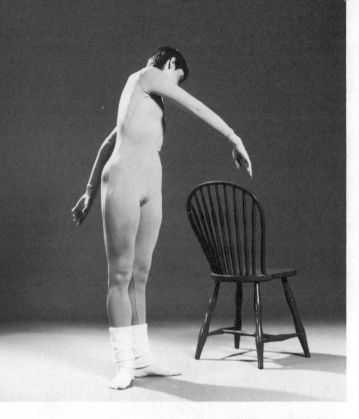

1. Lowering your head and stretching your neck toward your support, lean to the left, twisting your shoulder and torso in that direction. Your arms are fairly relaxed and your left arm swings back and your right arm swings to the front.

2. Swing your torso to the right so you're looking past your right foot. Your arms are still relaxed, left arm in front of you while your right arm swings to the rear.

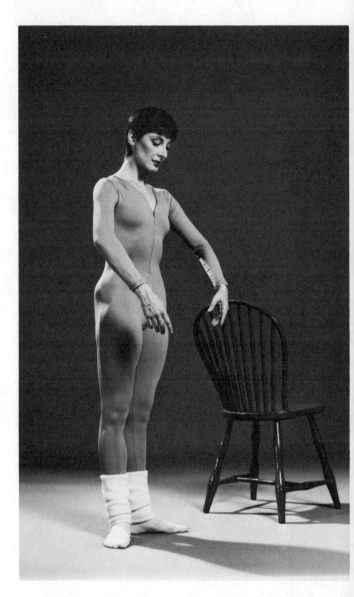

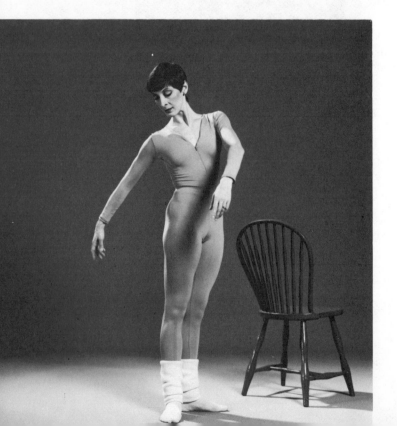

3. Swinging your torso to face forward, lift your head and both arms in front of you. Inhale deeply as you lift your arms above your head.

4. Circle your arms to the side, opening your chest, and lower both arms back to the starting position, exhaling as you lower them. Left hand holds support.

- Repeat the entire exercise of 16 counts in a reverse pattern, working your leg first **to the rear,** then **to the side,** and then **to the front.** The last 4 counts (torso swings) are repeated just as you did them the first time.

Repeat the entire exercise of 32 counts working the left side, holding the support with your right hand.

Exercise 11

This is an exercise that includes long leg stretches to the rear done while facing the support, as well as some side leg stretches. It also includes a turn, though a very simple one. You can practice using your spotting technique while doing this turn. In fact, I recommend that you practice spotting a few times before you even begin the exercise.

Tempo: A tango, as in "La Cumparsita" or "Hernando's Hideaway."

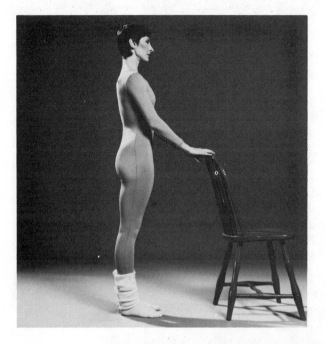

Starting Position: Stand facing the support with both hands resting on it, your heels together and feet parallel.

1, 2. Slowly stretching, lean your torso forward and bending your left knee, extend your right leg directly behind you as far as possible, toe pointed on the floor, keeping right leg straight and head down.

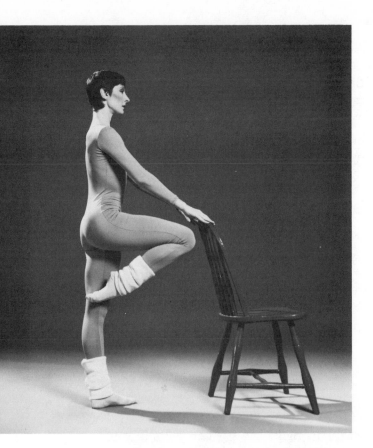

3. Straighten the left knee and, bringing your torso upright, bend your right knee and bring it forward, resting your pointed right toe on the side of your left knee. Your legs should not be turned out; they should face straight ahead.

4. Return to starting position.

5, 6, 7, 8. Repeat, stretching the left leg.

1. Leaning forward and bending your left knee, lift your right leg behind you, toe pointed, as high as you can.

2. Continue stretching your right leg behind you into the air, lifting it even higher.

3. Bringing your torso upright and straightening your left knee, bend your right knee and bring it forward, resting your pointed right toe on the side of your left knee.

4. Return to starting position.

5, 6, 7, 8. Repeat, lifting the left leg.

● Repeat first 8 counts (right and left leg stretch, keeping toe on floor).

Now you'll repeat the leg lifts to the rear, but this time pivoting after each one:

1. Leaning forward and bending your left knee, lift your right leg straight behind you, toe pointed, as high as you can.

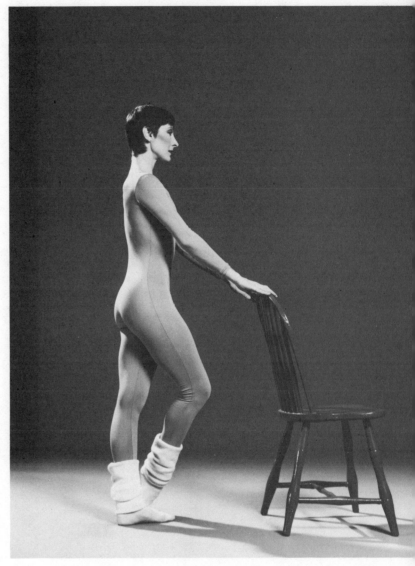

2. Bringing your torso upright and straightening your left knee, bend your right knee and bring it forward, resting your pointed right toe on the side of your left knee.

3. Put your right toe on the floor to the left of your left foot, then go up on the balls of your feet.

4. Releasing your support, pivot on your toes (don't forget to spot), at the last minute bringing your right foot back to the starting position and resting your hands on the support again.

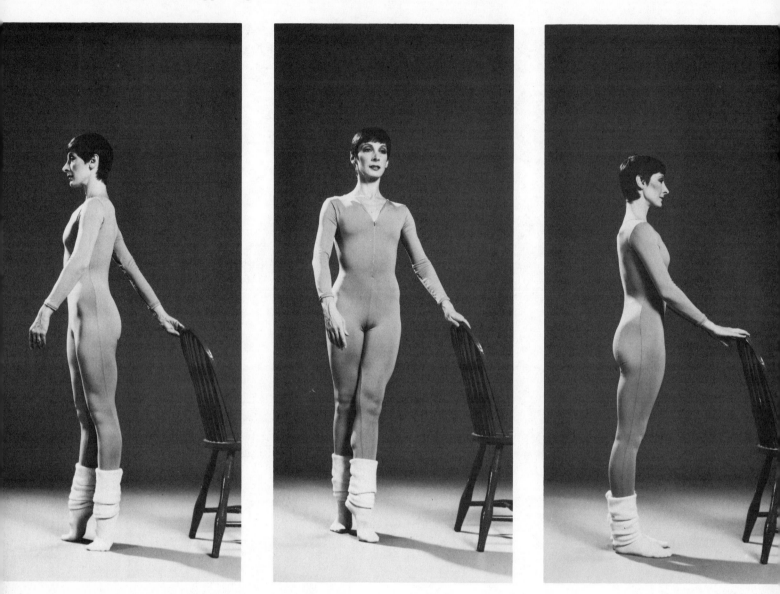

Now repeat these 4 counts with the other leg:

5. Leaning forward and bending your right knee, lift your left leg behind you, toe pointed, as high as your can.

6. Straightening your torso and your right knee, bend your left knee and bring it forward, resting your pointed left toe on the side of your right knee.

7. Put your left toe on the floor to the right of your right foot, then go up on the balls of your feet.

8. Releasing your support, pivot on your toes (don't forget to spot), at the last minute bringing your left foot back to the starting position and resting your hands on the support again.

Here's an optional stretching exercise you can do. In the previous combination you were stretching your legs to the back, and in this one you're stretching your legs to the side. When you grab your leg and lift it, the goal is to hold your ankle, but when you first do the exercise, that probably won't be possible. So just grab your leg wherever you can comfortably hold it: the calf or behind the knee or thigh.

Tempo: Same as the main exercise.

Starting Position: Stand facing the support, both hands on it, with ankles together and feet turned out as far as is comfortable.

1, 2. Bend your left knee and lift your right leg to the side with knee bent and toe pointed. Release your right arm from your support and grab your right knee. Gently pull it toward your body.

3, 4. Move your right hand and get hold of your right ankle or calf. Keeping your left knee bent, straighten the right leg so it's pointed to the side. Holding on, stretch the leg so it's lifted as high as possible.

5, 6. Straighten your left leg. Stretch the right leg just a bit more, trying for more height.

7, 8. Lower the right leg to the floor, brushing it into place. Return your right hand to the support.

- Repeat movement to a count of 8, working the left leg.
- Repeat both sides again, working the right leg for a count of 8 and then the left leg for a count of 8.

Exercise *12*

This exercise is a series of small jumps done while facing the support. It's good for strengthening the legs and also for developing flexibility. Remember while doing these jumps that the upper part of your body should remain as relaxed as possible. Try not to lift your shoulders or bend your waist. Your legs should be doing all the work. And there's no need to jump high—about 2 inches off the floor is right. The purpose of the jump is to use the feet and to get some aerobic activity.

Between jumps, your feet roll down to the floor. You should land on your toes but then roll gently down through the foot until the heel is down. This movement breaks and cushions the landing.

Tempo: This combination is done to a ragtime beat like the theme from *The Sting* by Scott Joplin, or to "Jingle Bells."

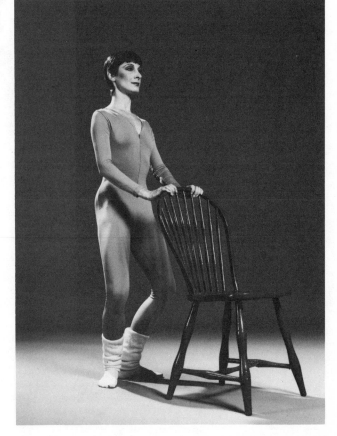

Starting Position: Stand facing the support, both hands resting on the support, heels together and feet turned out as far as is comfortable.

1. Bend both knees so they're directly over your feet.

111

2. Jump into the air, pointing your toes. Roll your feet down to the floor when you land until your heels are down, knees bent.

3. Repeat count 2.

4. Repeat count 2 again.

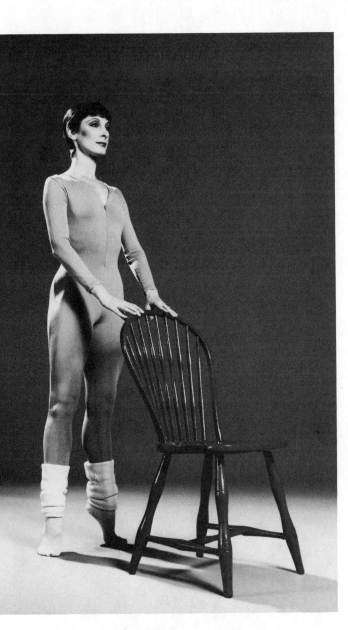

5. Rise onto the balls of your feet.

6. Lowering your heels to the floor, bend both knees into a plié.

7. Straighten both knees so you're back to the starting position.

8. Hold that position for one beat.

● Repeat this movement to a count of 8, but on the last count, keeping your heels on the floor, bend both knees into a plié in preparation for the next movement.

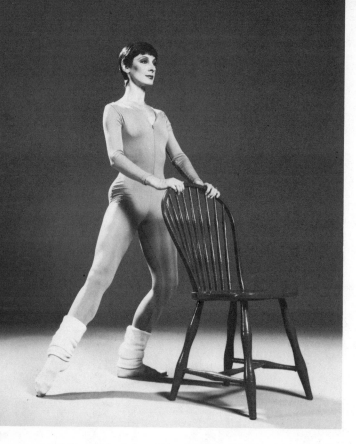

1. Extend right foot to the right, toe pointed and left leg bent, so your feet are about 12 inches apart.

2. Pushing off from the left foot, leap onto the right foot. ▲ Bring your left foot in to meet the right after you land. ▼

3. Now reverse the movement: Extend left foot to the left, toe pointed and right leg bent, so your feet are above 12 inches apart.

4. Pushing off from the right foot, leap onto the left foot. Bring your right foot in to meet the left after you land.

5, 6. Repeat counts 1 and 2.

7, 8. Repeat counts 3 and 4.

In this sequence of jumps, you land on the beat.

1. Jump straight up into the air, landing with your feet about 12 inches apart, rolling through your foot as you land, heels down, toes turned out, knees bent.

2. Repeat count 1.

3. Repeat again.

4. Repeat again.

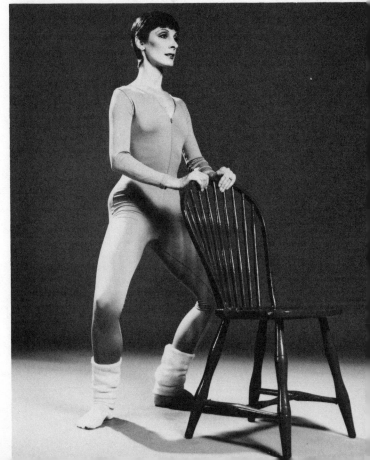

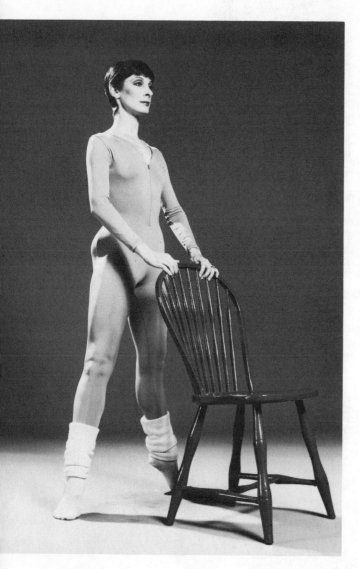

6, 7. Inhale deeply as you lift your arms gracefully to the side.

8. Lower your heels and your arms so you're back to the starting position.

5. Go up on the balls of your feet.

• Rest a few seconds and repeat the entire exercise again from the beginning.

Exercise 13

I think of this combination as "stork stretches" because you're standing on one leg and stretching the other. Remember to keep your body straight as you lift your foot behind you. Keep your knees together, buttocks tight and pelvis tucked in. You'll be tempted to sway your back, but don't! Pull up your abdominal muscles and breathe deeply.

In addition to the leg stretches, you'll also be doing body stretches away from and toward the support, which will help limber your spine and give you flexibility.

Tempo: Slow 4/4 time, as in "Stranger in Paradise."

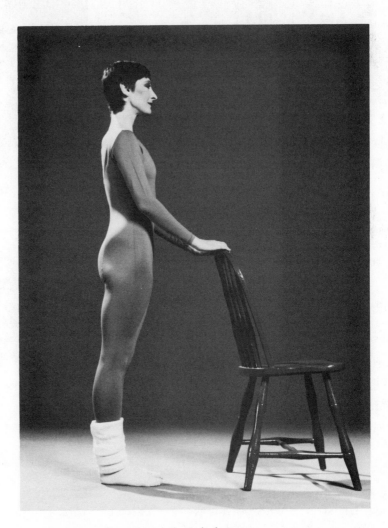

Starting Position: Stand facing your support with both hands resting on the support and feet parallel.

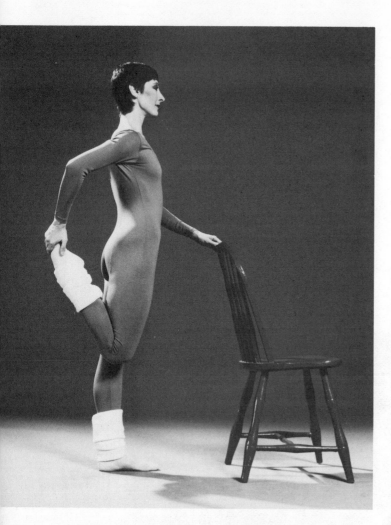

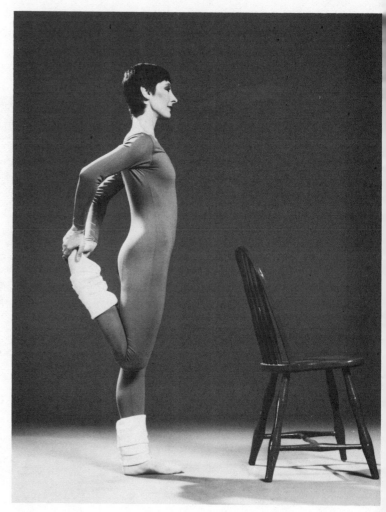

1. Bend your right knee and, keeping your knees together, lift your right foot behind you and grab it with your right hand.

2. Grab your right foot with your left hand as well, so that both hands are holding the foot behind you.

3. Gently pull the foot toward you, feeling the stretch in your thigh.

4. Return your right foot to the floor and both hands to the support.

- Repeat stretch with the other leg.
- Repeat the stretch with both legs—each to a count of 4—for a total count of 8.

1, 2, 3, 4. Putting your chin down and pulling away from the support, lean forward as far as you can, feeling the stretch in the back of your legs, your back and your shoulders. Keep your feet flat on the floor. Make sure your support is firmly anchored before you try this!

5, 6, 7, 8. Slowly roll up to the starting position.

1, 2, 3, 4. Pushing against the support, move your hips forward and bend backward, keeping your shoulders down and stretching your neck backward without losing control of your neck muscles.

5, 6, 7, 8. Slowly roll back up to the starting position.

● Repeat entire exercise from the beginning.

Exercise 14

Here at last is your deep bow done with a pointed toe, which finishes your exercises with a flourish. You'll also be doing a turn between bows and you'll need to spot again for that. While the bow looks quite graceful and is really fun to do, it's also a good stretch for your arms, back and legs.

Tempo: This is done to a waltz tempo or a 2/4 time, as in "Oh, What a Beautiful Morning."

Starting Position: Holding the support with your left hand, stand with your heels an inch or so apart, toes turned out only as far as is comfortable. Your right arm is relaxed at your side.

1. Lift your right arm to the side to just above shoulder height as you point your right toe forward, bending your left knee slightly.

2. Bend forward from the waist . . .

3. until your right hand nearly brushes your right foot (or is as low as you can comfortably reach).

4. Then, leading with the elbow, uncurl your body, watching your right hand . . .

5. as you begin to lift your arm forward and up.

6. Straighten your left leg and continue lifting your arm
until it's overhead and both legs are straight.

7. Put your right toe on the floor to the left of your left foot and go up on the balls of your feet.

125

8. Turning on the balls of your feet, replace your left hand on the support with your right and turn until you're facing the opposite direction from your original starting position.

Repeat entire movement, working your left arm and leg, to a count of 8.

Exercise Shorthand

Once you're familiar with the exercises and you have your technique down pat, you'll find it faster and easier to just follow this shorthand instead of turning the pages of the book. So here's a breakdown of each of the 14 exercises. I'd suggest that if you don't have a tape of music you've made for the exercises, you could just jot down the name of each song you hum next to the notes on each exercise.

1. Achilles stretch, shoulders and head.

2. Pliés, arm circles front and back, wider pliés, side arm stretch.

3. Bends forward with arm; points front, side, back; rise on balls of feet; bend all the way down; bend all the way side.

4. Weight change front; up on balls of feet; weight change side; bending knees, arms up; repeat back; repeat side.

5. Pick up knee and hold; point front, bend knee and flex foot, point and down, arm up; repeat to side and back; full forward bend with knees straight.

6. Brush forward twice; out, ankle, out, in; repeat side and back; 7 leg swings; 4 bent knee lifts; side brush to wide plié, up on balls of feet twice; 4 bent knee lifts; repeat all starting to back.

7. Brush front to bent knee; point and half circle around; brush front to bent knee and back to position; bend side pointing foot; change weight to bend away from support and return; repeat back.

8. Curl toward support, out straight, point on floor and return; twice to front, side, back; front curls bending inside knee, balls of feet, arm side; repeat starting back.

9. Raise leg on bent knee, straighten bringing foot to knee, point on floor, kick and return; repeat side and back; point foot front, leaning back; again back, side front; point foot back, leaning back.

10. Raise bent leg leaning toward support; open arm, straighten leg, return; repeat side and back; arm swings toward support and away, twisting body, then arms circle; again back, side, front; again swinging arm movements.

11. Face support and stretch right leg to rear, toe pointed on floor; repeat left; right toe off floor; left toe off floor; repeat all with turn at end. Optional leg stretch to side.

12. Small jumps.

13. Bring foot to bottom holding toes; repeat to other side; bend pulling from support; bend pushing into support; repeat whole thing.

14. Bow.

PART THREE

The Dance

The Dance

This dance is based on most of the exercises you've been doing at your support. It includes stretching, kicking, bending and turning. You should have fun doing it, and it's a terrific aerobic exercise. Once you're familiar with the entire dance, do it so one move flows into the next. The dance begins slowly and builds; you will have worked up quite a sweat by the time you're finished. Make sure as you move through the dance that you make the most of each movement. Remember all the tips I gave you about breathing and movement as you worked through the exercises. Smile while you dance and pretend that you have an audience; there's nothing like the feeling of a performance to help you bring your best to what you're doing.

I've choreographed the dance to the theme music from *Flashdance*, though you can do it to any music you choose. I'd suggest that you stick with strong music, like disco music, with a 2/4 beat—something that really makes you feel like dancing. The dance isn't very long—it takes about three minutes—but it's vigorous and will give you a good workout. I think it's best to do the dance after you've done at least some, if not all, of the basic stretching exercises. Whatever you do, don't attempt the dance without some kind of warm-up, whether it's my exercises or a series you've developed yourself; if you try the dance without letting your muscles warm up, you're liable to hurt yourself.

All of the steps in the dance, with one exception, are done to counts of eight, and the exception is two steps, each to a count of four.

I suggest that you "walk" yourself through the steps before you try to do them to music. And don't forget to concentrate on technique—the more control you use, the more effective the exercise.

Movement 1: Head Rolls

Starting Position: Stand with your arms relaxed at your sides, feet turned out as far as is comfortable and about 18 inches apart.

Head roll to the right:

1. Head forward and to right side.

2. Head back.

3. Head to left side.

4. Head forward.

Head roll to the left:

5. Head to left side.

6. Head back.

7. Head to right side.

8. Head forward, then to center.

Movement 2: Single Arm Circles

1, 2, 3, 4. Watching your hand, make a large circle with your right arm, stretching it across the front of your body to your left side, over your head, to your right side and then back to the starting position.

5, 6, 7, 8. Repeat arm circle with left arm.

Movement 3: Double Arm Circles

1, 2, 3, 4. Make a circle with both arms, reaching down in front of you, up over your head, and backward, then returning to the starting position.

5, 6, 7, 8. Reverse the circle you just made, reaching behind you, up over your head, in front of you and then down, back to the starting position.

Movement 4 and 5: Side Reaches

1, 2, 3, 4. Reach your right arm out to the side, leading with your elbow, your wrist, and finally your hand. Bend your right knee as you reach. Reach as far as you can, feeling the stretch. Return to the starting position.

5, 6, 7, 8. Reach your left arm out to the side, leading with your elbow, your wrist, and finally your hand. Bend your left knee as you reach. Reach as far as you can, feeling the stretch. Return to the starting position.

- Repeat the reach to the right to a count of 4.
- Repeat the reach to the left to a count of 4.

Movement 6: Leg and Arm Circles and Shoulder Rolls

1. Plié on your left leg as you pick up and bend right knee and swing your right arm across your body in a circle over your head.

2. Straighten your legs, right foot pointed, and take a big step onto the right foot, rolling the foot onto the floor and shifting your weight to the right leg as you point your left foot to the side.

3, 4. Repeat to the other side: Pick up and bend your left knee and swing your left arm in a circle over your head. Lift your left knee up in front of you and then out to the side. Straighten your leg, toes pointed, and take a big step onto the left foot, rolling the foot onto the floor and shifting your weight to the left leg.

5. Roll your right shoulder back as you bend your right knee and shift your weight to your right foot.

6. Roll your left shoulder back as you bend your left knee and shift your weight to your left foot.

7. Roll your right shoulder back as you bend your right knee and shift your weight to your right foot.

8. Roll your left shoulder back as you bend your left knee and shift your weight to your left foot.

NOTE: If you're doing the dance to the music of *Flashdance,* you must do a total of 8 rather than 4 shoulder rolls in order to make the counts work with the steps.

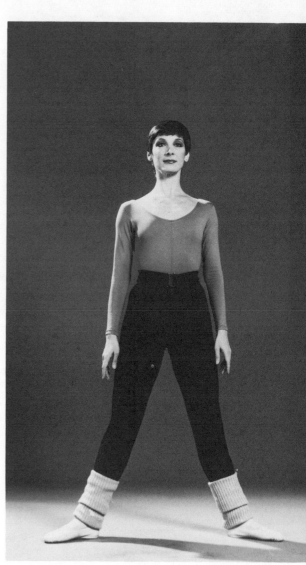

1, 2. Keeping your left knee bent, reach to your left with your right hand. Then straighten your leg as you return to starting position.

3, 4. Bend left knee and reach across your body with your right arm and swing your arm backward in an overhead circle. Straighten your leg and return to starting position.

5, 6. Bend your right knee, reach to your right with your left hand. Then straighten your leg as you return to starting position.

7, 8. Bend right knee and reach across your body
with your left arm and swing your arm backward
in an overhead circle. Straighten your leg and
return to starting position.

- Repeat cross reaches to the count of 8:
Reach, down, reach, circle; reach, down,
reach, circle.

1. Bending your left knee, reach across your body with your right arm, swinging your left arm behind you in the opposite direction.

2. Turning your body to the right as you bend your right knee, reach across your body with your left arm, swinging your right arm in the opposite direction behind you.

3 and 4. Do a "3-step walkaround" turn to your left in 2 counts: Step to the left with your left leg, then step to the left with your right leg, pivot turn, then step to the left with your left leg bent, right arm across your body.

5, 6, 7 and 8. Repeat this step to the other side.

● Repeat again to each side, for a total of 8 more counts.

Movement 10: Low Kicks

1. Bend both knees and then straighten them, kicking your right foot forward, twisting your upper body to the right as you kick. Put your right foot on the floor and bend both knees again.

2. Straighten your legs and kick the left foot forward, twisting your upper body to the left. Put your left foot on the floor and bend both knees again.

3. Straighten your legs and this time kick the right foot. As you kick it, turn your body to the left so the foot ends up being kicked behind you.

4. Step back onto your right foot, bring your left foot back and shift your weight to left foot. Take a step foward with your right foot, bending your knees, and

5, 6, 7, 8. Repeat kicks, this time starting with the left.

● Repeat the previous step to a count of 8—4 counts to each side—but this time kick as high as you can.

Movement 12 and 13: Arabesque

Now an arabesque to each side: Take 8 counts to do the following movement.

Step onto your right foot and extend your left leg to the back with toe pointed. Bending your right knee, put all your weight on your right foot.

Lean forward, lifting your left arm behind and your right arm in front of you as you lift your left leg behind you as high as you can.

Bend your left knee as you straighten your right knee, bringing your right arm up over your head.

Bring your pointed left toe across the front of your right knee, keeping your left knee pointing to the left.

Put your left foot on the floor across your right, and then pivot in place, bringing your right arm across your body.

● Step onto your left foot and repeat the arabesque to the other side to a count of 8.

1, 2, 3, 4. With feet apart and arms overhead, reach and stretch forward, bending over and all the way down to the floor until your hands reach the floor (or as close as you can get).

5, 6, 7, 8. Bend your right knee and put your weight on your right foot as you turn your torso to the right. Lifting your head, stretch both your arms back behind you, then make a giant circle with your arms, stretching over your head, then out over your right knee, then down. Straighten your right leg and bring your torso upright as you turn to the front again.

● Repeat front stretch and side circle-stretch to the left side for 8 counts.

Movement 16: Side Kick

You don't want to kick your leg very high. Just kick with lots of strength and taut muscles.

Bend both knees and then . . .

1. Straighten the left and kick the right leg forward while turning your torso to the right. Lower into a plié and . . .

2. Straightening both legs, kick the left leg while turning your torso to the left. Lower into a plié and . . .

3, 4. Repeat counts 1 and 2.

5, 6. Repeat again.

7, 8. Repeat again.

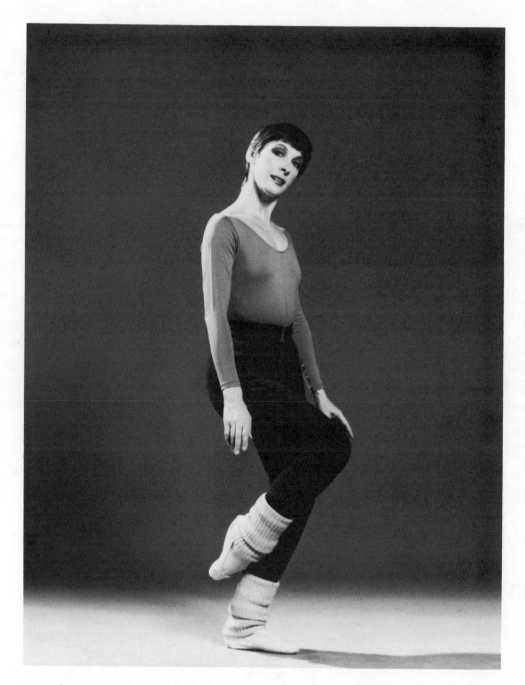

1, 2. Swing your bent right knee in front of your body and then kick it as high as you can to the right side, lifting your arms above your head as you kick.

3. Bring the right foot back to the floor and bend your right knee. Reach across your body with your left hand, stretching over the knee, down and toward the floor.

4. Now bend your left knee and reach across your body with your right hand, stretching toward the floor. ▼ Return to starting position.

5, 6, 7, 8. Repeat to the other side for 4 more counts.

1, 2. With your left knee bent and your right leg straight, turn your torso to the left and bend over, stretching your right arm in front of you and out as far as you can. Your left hand is on your hip.

3, 4. Make a large backward circle with your right arm, out, up and over your head, and finally behind you. Straighten your left knee and turn your torso forward.

5, 6, 7, 8. Repeat the movement to the other side, circling your left arm, for 4 more counts.

- Now repeat the entire movement, first to the left, then to the right, for a total of 8 additional counts.

Movements 20 and 21: Flings

Put lots of strength and energy into this movement. Fling your arms and twist your torso with vigor. Rise onto the balls of your feet and come down sharply.

1. Plié and rise onto the balls of your feet, stretching both straight arms up over your head.

2. Repeat first count: Lower into a plié, bringing your arms down, and rise onto the balls of your feet, stretching both arms straight up over your head.

3. Lower into a plié, bringing your arms down, then rise onto your toes, turning your torso to the left as you stretch your right arm into the air, your left arm behind you.

4. Lower into a plié, then rise onto the balls of your feet, turning your torso to the **right** as you stretch your left arm into the air, your right arm behind you.

5, 6, 7, 8. Repeat first 4 counts—two flings facing front, a stretch to the left and one to the right—for a total of 4 more counts.

● Repeat entire movement again for another 8 counts.

A Final Note...

I hope that you'll enjoy doing my ballet exercises for years. Once the steps are familiar, you'll be able to focus on your technique. But you may find that learning these exercises inspires you to try a ballet class. A weekly class combined with these exercises a few times a week will keep you in wonderful shape and the class can motivate you to keep working. And, of course, it's really fun to take a regular class—to dance with other people and to make friends with others who share your interest.

If you do decide to look for a ballet class in your area, here are some pointers to help in your selection:

One of the best ways to find a ballet class is to get a personal recommendation from someone who studies ballet and knows a good school in your area. Another source of information on ballet classes in your area is *Dance Magazine*. It has a section that gives information on schools all over the country. Finally, you can always check the Yellow Pages, but if you are relying on the phone book for the name of a school, be especially careful to check out the classes in person before you sign up.

No matter how you find a ballet school, you should make a point of visiting the school before you sign up.

Check out the studio. Is it licensed? Is it well run? Is there a feeling of organization about the place? Take note of the physical setup. The studio should have a wood floor; a cement floor is hard on the feet, legs and back. If the weather is cold, the studio should be adequately heated for both comfort and safety. The dance area should be uncluttered and large enough to handle the number of people in the class; you shouldn't have to worry about bumping into your neighbor while you work.

Make sure you visit a class yourself. Make a point of going to see the class you would be in. Some schools will let you take a sample class, which is an excellent idea if you can manage it. In any event, you should at least be able to sit in on a class, if only briefly.

Watch the class. Is the level of competence of the students relatively equal? If the school mixes raw beginners with more advanced students, everyone suffers. Is there a good feeling in the class itself? A ballet class shouldn't be deadly serious, but I don't think class is the place for casual conversation. It's very distracting and it somehow seems unprofessional. Look at the students as the class is in progress. Do they have good basic alignment and coordination? Some classes stress movement for its own sake, and that isn't really ballet—it's aerobics. A good ballet class is serious about the basics. Make sure that the class includes a good, slow warm-up. A one-hour class should have at least a twenty-minute warm-up. In most of the classes I take we spend a half hour at the barre to warm up before we do any work on the floor.

Assess the teacher. He or she must have the right mental attitude and one that inspires you. There are some wonderful teachers that I'm simply not comfortable with and I avoid working with them. Ballet teachers should also have good credentials. Where did they study? Have they ever performed? It's not essential for a teacher to have studied at the best schools and performed around the world. But ballet is an art and there is no point in taking classes from someone who is an amateur. Watch how the teacher gives corrections and how much personal attention she or he gives to each student. A good teacher is aware of every student in the class and is interested in seeing everyone improve. Make sure the teacher's explanations and demonstrations are clear and easy for you to follow.

Remember that dance is for exercise, but it is also therapeutic. The right class should help you develop grace and coordination, and a good teacher should be able to guide you toward that goal.

Finally, remember that class should be fun. You should look forward to going and you should feel both pleasantly tired and exhilarated when class is over.

Whether you go on to take classes or not, I hope that this book has inspired you to savor the joys of ballet, as both a participant and an observer.